Hora de cenar

por Barbara L. Luciano
ilustrado por Ginna Magee

Scott Foresman
is an imprint of

Glenview, Illinois • Boston, Massachusetts • Chandler, Arizona
Upper Saddle River, New Jersey

Every effort has been made to secure permission and provide appropriate credit for photographic material. The publisher deeply regrets any omission and pledges to correct errors called to its attention in subsequent editions.

Unless otherwise acknowledged, all photographs are the property of Pearson.

Photo locations denoted as follows: Top (T), Center (C), Bottom (B), Left (L), Right (R), Background (Bkgd)

Illustrations by Ginna Magee

Photograph 8 Corbis

ISBN 13: 978-0-328-53290-2
ISBN 10:   0-328-53290-8

Copyright © by Pearson Education, Inc., or its affiliates. All rights reserved. Printed in the United States of America. This publication is protected by copyright, and permission should be obtained from the publisher prior to any prohibited reproduction, storage in a retrieval system, or transmission in any form or by any means, electronic, mechanical, photocopying, recording, or likewise. For information regarding permissions, write to Pearson Curriculum Rights & Permissions, One Lake Street, Upper Saddle River, New Jersey 07458.

Pearson® is a trademark, in the U.S. and/or other countries, of Pearson plc or its affiliates.

Scott Foresman® is a trademark, in the U.S. and/or other countries, of Pearson Education, Inc., or its affiliates.

2 3 4 5 6 7 8 9 10 V0N4 13 12 11 10

Mis dos caballos grandes tienen hambre.

La gallina y sus cuatro pollitos comen maíz aquí.

El chancho grande come de todo.

Ya son las cinco en punto.

¡Qué bueno está todo hoy!

Modos de moverse

Leamos juntos

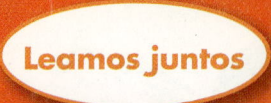

Todos los animales de este libro comen. Los animales también se mueven. Cada animal tiene un modo especial de moverse. Algunos animales caminan porque tienen patas. Algunos nadan con aletas. ¡Hay algunos que saltan! ¿De qué otros modos se mueven los animales?

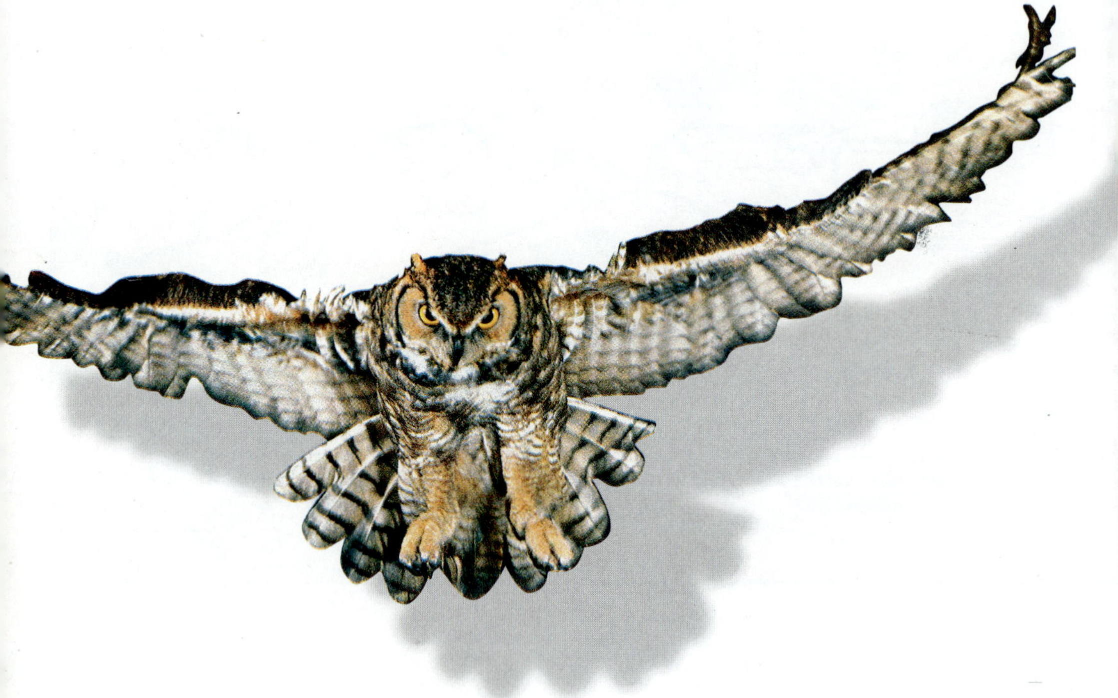